Super Lou!

A Memoir

Marcia Elise Wolfson

Dear Mark and Janet — Being made into film — Thanks for ... Enjoy — Marcia Wolfson

Super Lou!

A Memoir

Marcia Elise Wolfson

Waterfront Digital Press

My amazing son and his precious family. Words cannot explain what Alan is. He has made me want to live, and gone through my Peaks and Valleys 5777 Borach Ashem.

To my brother Steve Wolfson and Barbara, his loving wife. To Gary Wolfon, and his devoted wife Marisa. To Nathan Wolfson, and sweet Sylvia.

To my Uncle Nathan Wolfson. Cousins Joy Jerden, Donna Schmidt, Jordan Avery Foster, John and Joan Monsky. To my dear friend Lisa Sutherland. To Dr. Morton Aronson, who helped me survive it all.

To Stephen Paul Wolfson, my rock. To Gary Wolfson, my hope. To Martin Wolfson, my baby brother. To Daniel Drake, my husband, who has stuck by me through ups and downs – Daniel Drake ... with love. To Abby Bergman, the wonderful editor. To Louise Reynolds, a lovely friend. To Ken Fraser, the terrific designer.

To Dr. Margaret Stanley, Coo Coo and Goldie – the world behind me. Whose Life is it Anyway?

tilt

Dedicated to my wonderful Mother, Aunt Hazel, and Emily Wurn; three women who influenced my life.

Marcia Wolfson

I am lopsided. I am smart
but live in an upside-down world.
This makes me feel stupid It makes me
eat wrongly sleep wrongly love
wrongly and probably die wrongly
Oh Soul, just go on a little longer
to solve what you are due on
earth. Maybe being hungry being hurt
misunderstood has made me grow-

I could be a rose, but I am covered
With thorns-ouch-everyone looks

at me like the court jester. But tilted
world. I am a princess inside
I was raised like royalty-not a bag
Lady in New York.
Yes, this happened step by step–
no one can see the flower-only
Its thorns–
Tilt like a pinball machine–
be straight–don't tilt–be that
princess.

preface

My Roller Coaster life began over five decades ago. When I had wedding of the Year in Colliers Magazine; the wedding was beautiful. It was in our Miami home, with orchids floating in pool with crystal swans, crystal chandeliers in the huge tent facing Biscayne Bay.

The beginning. This marriage to Everett Lassman, owner of Wolfie's Restaurant, lasted three years with two miscarriages, and my going to a rehabilitation center in Stockbridge, Massachusetts for depression. After a 30-day stay, we divorced and I moved to New York City. Daddy was the center of my life, and Mother was the sweetest, most wonderful Mother in the world. Though I was Daddy's "little shug," short for sugar. I had three darling younger brothers.

Our lifestyle was how I read about now – lavish beyond words. Life in Beverly Hills California at the Beverly Hills

Hotel Bungalow, Mansion next door to LBJ on beautiful Ellicott Street when Dad owned the Transit System in D.C; Apartment at Pierre Hotel in Manhattan, and our incredible home in Miami Beach. I then met and married my second husband Rabbi Manfred Rechtschaffen. My incredible son and his wonderful family who make my life complete. My Mother died in 1968, at this time Daddy went to prison, and I filed for my second divorce in which I had a tremendous custody battle. I won. But I was banished and miserable.

My downward spiral began after 1968, when Super Lou demanded we move to London, England. There I married a third time. I was panic stricken, and married an Italian director, Michael Daddio. Daddy would not speak anymore. I was further depressed and heartbroken, and lived because of my darling Alan. We returned from the U.K. in 1980, when Alan and I moved to Jacksonville, Florida – my hometown. Daddy would send me no money unless I lived there.

I worked in Public Relations, and as kindergarten teacher until my world crumbled in 1982. We returned to New York. I divorced from Michael and began teaching and Alan continued to be the center of my world. In 1987 after much volatile living, Daddy still not speaking, Alan 19-years-old, I met and married Dan Drake. That was 30 years ago...

Alan's wedding in 2000 gave me the strength to confront my Father. We both cried, and the mending of our Father-Daughter relationship began. It's when I began writing Super Lou, bringing us up until today 2016. This is my capsule version – Marcia Elise Wolfson.

overview

The true story of Louis Elwood Wolfson is an All-American saga of ambition, greed, scandal, and redemption with echoes of "Citizen Kane" and "There Will Be Blood." The child of Jewish immigrants born in 1912, Wolfson literally fought his way to the top, first as a professional boxer, and later as a political kingmaker and ruthless financier who riled up Wall Street by pioneering hostile corporate takeovers while amassing one of the greatest personal fortunes in the post-World War II era. Upon Wolfson's death in 2007, Henry G. Manne, dean of George Mason University School of Law, memorialized his pivotal role in American history by declaring that "Wolfson's contribution to human welfare far exceeded the total value of all private philanthropy in history. He invented the modern hostile-tender offer. This invention, which activated and energized the market for corporate control, was the primary cause of the revolutionary restructuring of American Industry in the 1970's and '80's, and the ensuing economic boom."

Wolfson's sharp intellect, double-sided personality, and vast range of financial, political, and sporting interests made him a larger than life character who was capable of charming his bitterest business rivals and betraying those dearest to him, most especially the members of his own family. Born in St. Louis in 1912, Wolfson was the son of a junk dealer from Lithuania who escaped conscription into the Russian army and fled to the United States. A Hollywood handsome professional pugilist who fought under the name "Kid Wolf" and a star football player, he was raised in Jacksonville, Florida. He dropped out of the University of Georgia after an injury ended his college football career, and used $15,000 borrowed from his family and a Georgia football fan to buy a derelict farm owned by the J.C. Penney family that was littered with junk and metal pipe. He leveraged that purchase into a building supply company that made him a millionaire by age 28. In 1946, at age 34, he began making his mark as a major philanthropist whose example would later be emulated by the likes of Bill Gates and Warren Buffett, with a donation of $500,000, the equivalent of $6 million in today's dollars, to what became the Wolfson Children's Hospital in Jacksonville.

In 1949, Wolfson made the first successful hostile takeover of a prominent American corporation by seizing control of Capital Transit, which provided bus service in Washington, DC. His insistence on paying the first dividends ever awarded to the company's shareholders earned him acclaim from investors and enmity from entrenched national and local politicians who purported to champion average riders. In the early 1950s, Wolfson transformed Merritt-Chapman & Scott (MCS), a mid-sized marine construction firm, into one of the nation's first conglomerates, winning high profile contracts to build the Glen Canyon Dam in Arizona, the Navy super-carrier Kitty Hawk, and the Mackinac Bridge linking Michigan's upper and lower peninsulas. In 1955, he gained national publicity with an attempted hostile takeover of Montgomery Ward and a bid to gain control of George Romney's American Motors.

Though both the Montgomery Ward and American Motors deals were ultimately unsuccessful, the bold overtures by "the Junkman from Florida" shook up the eastern establishment and entrenched corporate management, ushered in a new age of corporate raids on Wall Street whose legacy later inspired "junk bond" king Michael Milken, T. Boone Pickens, and present day moguls like Carl Icahn. A 1955 New York Times article headlined "Today's Giants of Finance" ranked Wolfson alongside Texas oil tycoon H.L. Hunt and Howard Hughes. He consorted with celebrities like Marilyn Monroe and Joe DiMaggio (his younger brother Cecil's best friend), Mickey Mantle, Roger Maris, Nat King Cole, Lauren Bacall, and Frank Sinatra. He also developed valuable "friends in high places," including Tennessee senator Al Gore Sr., whose annual cattle auctions garnered suspiciously high bids from political supporters and patronage seekers like the Wolfson brothers.

Wolfson's status as one of the post-war era's most highly publicized businessmen proved to be a double edged sword. In the wake of his corporate raids, some investors acclaimed his as a Robin Hood, while critics branded him a robber baron and a criminal. His bid for Montgomery Ward sparked kidnapping threats that prompted the F.B.I to send agents to guard him and his family. His wheeling and dealing in American Motors and other companies also attracted scrutiny from the Securities and Exchange Commission, which launched a series of investigations that outside observers later claimed were overzealous and tinged with anti-Semitism. Wolfson nevertheless went on to accumulate interests in oil, movie theaters, and newspaper publishing (Jacksonville Chronicle, Miami Beach Sun), becoming a liberal Democrat counterpart to Hunt, Hughes, and William Randolph Hearst. He later co-financed Mel Brook's first movie, "The Producers," – a meeting which Steve Wolfson was the force behind – after insisting that Brooks act out each part for him. His celebrity status was confirmed and elevated by splashy profiles and numerous articles in Time, Life, Business Week, Fortune, and the Wall Street Journal, as well as in the New York Times.

Inevitably, Wolfson's rise to fame and financial fortune was marred by a series of major scandals. In 1955, he was named by the Kefauver committee's organized crime investigation report as a major contributor to an allegedly corrupt Florida governor associated with local gambling rings. In the late 1960's, he was convicted of two felonies related to securities transactions. The latter of those felony convictions resulted in him serving a nine-month imprisonment in a federal penitentiary. During this same period, Wolfson was the subject of lurid national headlines involving his alleged bribery of

Supreme Court justice Abe Fortas, a scandal that led to Fortas's resignation in 1969. Wolfson was also accused of making suspect payments to President Richard Nixon's attorney general John Mitchell and to Kennedy assassination investigating New Orleans District attorney Jim Garrison. An offshoot of both affairs was an alleged grand larceny plot against Wolfson by broadcaster Larry King, whom Wolfson got arrested only to be informed that the statute of limitations on King's alleged crimes had expired. Following his incarceration for the aforementioned felony conviction, Wolfson became an advocate for prison reform, and an even more active philanthropist who contributed millions of dollars to medical, educational, and religious charities in his hometown of Jacksonville.

Ironically, Wolfson managed to achieve his last great acclaim through thoroughbred horse racing. His first foray into the sport of kings began in 1960 when he purchased Harbor View Farms near Ocala, Florida. He quickly proceeded to establish northern Florida as the upstart rival of traditional thoroughbred capitals like Kentucky and Maryland. In 1979 Harbor View Farms gave birth to a weanling christened Affirmed. The choice of the colt's name was an apparent reference to the legal term denoting a positive court judgment. At the time, Wolfson was still struggling to recover from financial setbacks that included the loss of control of some of his major corporate interests and legal defense bills that totaled over $10 million. In a series of epic 1978 races against the favored Alydar, Affirmed won the Triple Crown, a feat that has not since been duplicated, and was voted Horse of the Year in 1978 and 1979. Along with direly needed prize money and immense personal satisfaction, Affirmed's historic victories earned Wolfson at least partial redemption from his alleged sins on the business and political fronts.

Along the way, Wolfson's personal life became fraught with internecine conflict exacerbated by tabloid style dalliances. The father of a daughter and three sons, he was so tyrannical, controlling, and narcissistic around his family that his offspring began referring to him as "Daddy Dearest," the male equivalent of Joan Crawford. He had close friendships and/or romances with Hollywood and media celebrities including Hedy Lamarr, Deborah Kerr, Zsa Zsa Gabor, Debbie Reynolds, and Barbara Walters. His first wife, Florence Monsky Wolfson, died of cancer in 1968. Wolfson later wed Patrice Jacobs, the daughter of a Hall of Fame horse trainer. Upon his death in 2007 at age 95, he bequeathed the bulk of his fortune to Patrice and his favorite charities, and relative pittances to the children of his first wife, a legacy that devolved into will contests and bittersweet memories for all concerned.

JUNKMAN GENIUS will present a definitive biographical portrait of Louis Wolfson, showing him warts and all but giving him credit where due, while recreating the tumultuous political and social atmosphere of his heydays from the 1940's to the late 1970's. Author Marcia Wolfson, the eldest child of his first wife, will draw on extensive family archives, and interviews with Wolfson's secretary, Louise Reynolds; actor/director Mel Brooks; former prosecutor Robert Morgenthau; his friend/ nemesis Larry King; friends and paramours like Debbie

Reynolds, Lauren Bacall, and Barbara Walters; and family members Marty Wolfson, Nathan Wolfson, Hazel Wolfson, and Richard Wolfson.

Competition and Marketing

There is no competing biography of Louis E. Wolfson, authorized or unauthorized, and no indication that anyone else is now or has in the past attempted to write one. Notoriously press-shy, especially following his incarceration in federal prison in 1970, Wolfson never granted any in depth interviews to outsiders during his life. However, he was well-known to the general public from the late 1940's through the late 1970's, most particularly in connection with his controversial takeover of the Washington, DC transit system; his corporate raids on Montgomery Ward, American Motors, and other companies; the scandal that led to the resignation of Supreme Court Justice Abe Fortas; his role in producing Hollywood films such as "The Producers;" his friendship with leading movie stars, sports figures, and celebrities of his era; and his thoroughbred Affirmed's victory in the 1978 Triple Crown races.

Wolfson was profiled in a splashy Life Magazine article in 1955. That same year, a New York Times article titled "Today's Giants of Finance" ranked him with the likes of H.L. Hunt and Howard Hughes. He was quoted in and/or prominently mentioned in literally hundreds of newspaper and magazine articles in the New York Times, the Wall Street Journal, the Washington Post, publications throughout his home state of Florida, Fortune, Business Week, Time, and Sports illustrated. He is also thumbnail profiled and/or prominently mentioned in several popular books about the history of American finance and books about horse racing history. Moreover, Wolfson's many legal battles are documented in numerous law review articles, including a 2011 monograph by St. Louis University law professor Alan M. Weinberger, who notes that, "Principal cases involving Wolfson appear in virtually all Corporation and Securities Regulation casebooks."

This prodigious body of material and the range of Wolfson's myriad interests and celebrity suggest that the marketing of JUNKMAN GENIUS should be targeted at such audiences as: (a) general interest readers fascinated by the finance, politics, and popular culture of the post-World War II period extending from the late 1940's through the 1970's; (b) readers interested in pioneering American financial figures who influenced junk bond kings like Michael Milken and corporate raiders like T. Boone Pickens; (c) aficionados of horse racing; (d) readers interested in the history of Hollywood and film celebrities; (e) scholars of Jewish history and assimilation into American culture; and (e) legal scholars with a special interest in securities regulation.

Here is a brief list of some notable books and law review articles referencing Wolfson:

The White Sharks of Wall Street: Thomas Mellon Evans and the Original Corporate Raiders, Diana B. Henriques (2000)

Dangerous Dreamers: The Financial Innovators from Charles Merrill to Michael Milken, Robert Sobel (1993)

Fortas; The Rise and Ruin of a Supreme Court Justice, Bruce Allen Murphy (1988)

Power Shift: The Rise of the Southern Him and its Challenge to the Eastern Establishment, Kirkpatrick Sale (1975)

Lawyer: A Life of Counsel and Controversy, Arthur L. Liman (1988) 7

Edward Bennett Williams for the Defense, Robert Pack (1983) A

The Man to See: Edward Bennett Williams - Legendary Lawyer, Ultimate Insider; Evan Thomas (1992)

Rearview Mirror: Looking Back at the FBI, the CIA, and Other Tales, William W. Turner (2001)

The Brethren: Inside the Supreme Court, Bob Woodward and Scott Armstrong (1996)

The Names They Give Them, J.B. Faulconer (1998)

Affirmed: The Last Triple Crown Winner, Lou Sahadi and Steve Cauthen (2011)

Affirmed and Alydar: Racing's Greatest Rivalry, Timothy T. Capps (2007)

"What's in a Name? The Tale of Louis Wolfson's Affirmed," Alan M. Weinberger (Hofstra Law Review, Volume 39, Issue 3, January 1, 2011)

"Cash Tender Offers for Shares – A reply to Chairman Cohen," Henry G. Manne (Duke Law Review, 1967)

table of contents

one | run for the rosebuds (may 6, 1978)

Louis Elwood Wolfson arrives at Churchill Downs under a dark cloud he longs to lift once and for all. It is shortly after 8 o'clock on the morning of May 6, 1978, five hours before the starting bell for the 104th Kentucky Derby, the fabled thoroughbred horse race known as "The Run for the Roses." Wolfson, age 66, strides into the paddock wearing a dark blue suit and the same poker-faced expression that has masked his public persona during his star crossed career as the former junkman and financial genius who became America's first corporate raider. Six feet tall with piercing steel blue eyes and a thicket of silvering brown hair, he is still as trim and almost as physically fit as the professional boxer and star football player he had been in high school and college. But in the wake of two convictions for securities violations that sent him to federal prison for nine months in 1969 and decimated his once proud financial empire, he has been branded a felon, a criminal, a jailbird.

The 1978 Kentucky Derby is far more than a horse race for Lou Wolfson - it is his chance for redemption from all his alleged sins, a moment with echoes of the rosebud scene in "Citizen Kane." All of Wolfson's hopes are pinned on an undersized second ranked contender named Affirmed. His jockey is an 18-year-old prodigy named Stevie Cauthen. As he visits his horse and jockey in the paddock, his life flashes before his eyes...

Herewith, Chapter One sets the tone and texture of the book by painting a vivid scene of Lou Wolfson at the 1978 Kentucky Derby, followed by teaser paragraphs that outline what the ensuing narrative will cover and segue into a flashback to his youth and the personality shaping saga of his forebears...

two | kid wolf (1912-1945)

Chapter Two starts with the birth in 1879 of a "Kid Wolf" in Lithuania named Morris David Wolfson, the father of Louis Wolfson. It describes the larger plight of Jews in Lithuania during the late 19th Century, and the socio-economic and political circumstances in eastern Europe and the world in general. It recounts the efforts of the Russian army to conscript Jewish boys like Morris Wolfson into military service, and Morris's daring escape to America at age 17. Landing in Baltimore, Maryland, Morris finds his first employment as a lowly clothes presser. He marries Sarah Goldberg, who has also fled Lithuania with her family. The Wolfsons migrate to St. Louis, Missouri, where Morris works as an iceman and a fruit-peddler. Sarah gives birth to a daughter, Irene, and a son, Sam, the first two of nine children, one of whom dies in infancy.

On January 28, 1912, Louis Elwood Wolfson is born in St. Louis. A short time later, Morris moves the family to Jacksonville, Florida, where he becomes a junkman and scrap metal dealer. This move is put in the documented historical context of Jewish life in the American South during this period. Not coincidentally, the famous stock market crash of 1929 occurs when Louis Wolfson is 17, the same age at which his father fled from Lithuania. At the urging of his older brother Sam, the athletically gifted Lou becomes a professional boxer who fights under the name "Kid Wolf" for $5 a bout. When Morris finds out what his sons are up to, he orders them to quit the boxing game and go back to school. Lou shows his leadership, charisma, and athletic gifts by becoming a high school football, basketball, baseball, and track star.

In 1930, amid the ever worsening Great Depression, Lou enrolls at the University of Georgia. He is a "salaried football player" whose tuition and living expenses are paid for by avid alumni like Harold Hirsch. Lou already recognizes that football is more than a sport: it is also a potential path to making money. By his Sophomore year, Lou becomes Georgia's starting right end. Then comes a crucial turning point. In the fall 1931 game against Yale, Lou suffers a serious shoulder injury while tackling Albie Booth, the All American running back, on the second half kickoff. That ends Lou's promising football career. But "Kid Wolf" is not out of luck: his appreciative benefactor is ready and willing to step up and support his future endeavors.

In 1932, Lou Wolfson embarks on what will prove to be a storied business career with the help of family and friends. He gets a $5,000 loan from Harold Hirsch and borrows another $10,000 against his father's insurance policies to start Florida Pipe and Supply Company. The firm is basically an incorporated junk dealer. Lou buys a derelict property 25 miles west of Jacksonville that's littered with pipe and scrap metal from the J.C. Penney family. The Depression has depressed prices, so he pays only $250. When the market rises again, he sells the "junk" on the property for $100,000.

In 1934, Lou's older brother Sam marries Sylvia Lehman, a Jewish Belle from Montgomery, Alabama. Lou falls in love with the bride's sister Florence, the maid of honor, who bears a striking resemblance to Maureen O'Hara. Several months later, Lou proposes by the river in Jacksonville. "Flo, sugar, I'm gonna give you the world. I love you with all my heart. Will you marry me?" The answer is yes. They wed in Montgomery in 1935. At the wedding, Lou's younger brother Saul meets his own future bride, Hazel Monsky, Flo's younger sister.

Lou makes good on his promise to give Flo the world. Though he is only the third oldest child, he is the family business leader, the pied piper. Older brother Sam and younger brothers Cecil, Saul, and Nathan all go to work for him selling pipe and scrap metal. "Lou always had a strong desire to be a winner, which came from sports," Nathan Wolfson recalls. "He transferred that desire to business. He'd set a goal for himself and he'd go out and achieve it." By 1940, with the Great Depression finally easing, Florida Pipe and Supply boasts annuals sales of $4.5 million. Lou Wolfson is a millionaire at the age of 28.

The Wolfson empire continues to prosper with America's entry into World War II as demand for pipe and scrap metal booms. While his brothers join the military, Lou remains in Jacksonville, classified as 4F due to his football injury and a bad kidney. He uses his vantage point to eye properties that will make him still more millions when the war ends.

three | the junkman cometh (1946-1953)

Lou Wolfson plunges into the postwar frenzy with a pair of deals that will shape his controversial public image as "the Junkman from Florida" for decades to come. In 1946, he buys the St. Johns River shipyard, which the Navy has spent $19 million developing, for lust $1.95 million. A short time later, he buys the Tampa Shipyard for $1.92 million. Government officials somehow fail to insert the standard requirement in the contracts that the winner bidder operate the yards rather than dismantle them. Selling the war surplus materiel piece by piece, Wolfson goes on to reap a $10 million profit from the two shipyard deals. Not surprisingly, the deals spark allegations of bribery followed by a congressional investigation and a grand jury inquiry. Happily for Wolfson, the probes eventually fizzle out, but from then on he is a marked man. In what critics will call a blatant attempt to burnish his image through philanthropy, Wolfson donates $500,000 to found the Wolfson Children's Hospital in Jacksonville, the equivalent of $6 million in today's dollars.

In 1947, Wolfson makes his first foray into the movie business with the purchase of a theater chain. The following year, he produces "The Babe Ruth Story" starring William Bendix and Claire Trevor. By now, Lou and Flo are the parents of three sons and a daughter, but the handsome and dashing Junkman can't help being tempted by Hollywood sirens like Hedy Lamarr, whom he meets at the Rose Bowl game in Pasadena, California.

Even so, Wolfson remains intensely focused on finance, much to the annoyance of WASP rivals in the eastern establishment. In 1949, he makes business history by launching the first ever hostile tender offer, a $2.2 million bid for control of Capital Transit, the firm that provides bus service in Washington, DC. He quickly replaces the board of directors and senior management and installs himself as chairman. But instead of investing in needed new equipment, he begins dispensing the company's whopping $6.7 million cash hoard to shareholders. Wolfson's management of Capital Transit is seen by critics as a classic case of "milking" by an absentee owner. The Washington Post editorializes that his tactics are "a hark-back to the robber baron days of the last century." Undaunted, Wolfson notes that Capital Transit never paid dividends to its investors prior to his tenure as chairman, and proudly proclaims that the interests of shareholders in a company should always come first.

On the heels of the Capital Transit tender, Wolfson invests $8 million in a take-over of Merritt-Chapman & Scott (MCS), a mid-sized marine construction firm. He quickly proceeds to make more business history by creating America's first conglomerate, adding public works, steel making, paint production, and even money lending subsidiaries-tome core shipbuilding enterprise. If his Florida shipyard deals made him a marked man, the Capital Transit and MCS deals effectively stamp a bull's eye on his back. In 1951, Tennessee senator Estes Kefauver conducts hearings into organized crime activity with a particular focus on the Florida underworld. The Kefauver Committee report names Wolfson as a contributor to the campaign of a local politician with ties to the mafia. But as Wolfson slyly notes, he has been developing his own "friends in high places." His brother Cecil is a regular bidder at the cattle auctions held by Tennessee's other senator, Albert Gore, Sr., where Gore livestock is snapped up by "friends" like the Wolfsons for suspiciously high prices. Further burnishing his image as a philanthropist, Lou establishes the charitable Wolfson Family Foundation in Jacksonville.

four | corporate raider (1954-1955)

Nothing captures the attention of the American public in 1954 quite like the whirlwind marriage and subsequent quickie divorce of New York Yankee baseball legend Joe DiMaggio and movie star Marilyn Monroe. Lou Wolfson knows both members of the happy/unhappy couple: brother Cecil is DiMaggio's best friend. Thanks to his film production activities and his passionate interest in sports, Lou also hobnobs with the likes of Mickey Mantle, Frank Sinatra, Lauren Bacall, Deborah Kerr, and Nat King Cole. Moreover, he is on the cusp of becoming a major business celebrity in his own right. In August, he launches a proxy contest for control of Montgomery Ward, the nation's second largest catalogue retailer behind Sears, Roebuck & Co. Much like Capital Transit, Montgomery Ward is hoarding cash, a staggering $300 million, and under stodgy management led by octogenarian chairman Sewell Lee Avery. "Montgomery Ward, as it stands today, is a glaring and notorious example of private enterprise in reverse gear," Wolfson declares at the announcement press conference.

The fight for control of Montgomery Ward quickly escalates into what the New York Times describes as "one of the fiercest battles in the history of corporate finance." In essence, it is a struggle to win the hearts and minds of the company's shareholders, or as Wolfson puts it, a war on behalf of "corporate democracy." Avery enlists his 2,000 employees to contact shareholders and persuade them to vote for management. Citing the Florida shipyard and Capital Transit deals, his minions attack Wolfson personally, branding him "an irresponsible raider" intent on "looting" the company. Wolfson embarks on his own barnstorming tour, traveling to shareholder meetings in California, New York, Chicago, Detroit, and Florida. If the Wolfson name does not become a household word on a par with DiMaggio and Monroe, his exploits are celebrated and documented by a splashy Life Magazine profile and scores of articles in Fortune, Business Week, the Wall Street Journal, and the business pages of the New York Times. After he gets anonymous phone calls threatening kidnapping, Wolfson, his wife, and children are put under the protection of the FBI.

The Montgomery Ward proxy war comes to a head on April 22, 1955, at a shareholders meeting at the Medinah Temple, a Shriners auditorium in Chicago.

Shrugging off the board of directors attempt to restrain him, chairman Avery insists on answering questions from the floor, often rambling on incoherently. Wolfson keeps his cool, believing that Avery is losing credibility. But old man Avery shrewdly implies that he will resign regardless of the outcome of the proxy fight, a promise he will ultimately keep. When the ballots are tallied, Wolfson wins just 30 percent of the vote. That's enough to gain three seats on the board, but not enough to win control. It is a Pyrrhic victory at best that has cost him half a million dollars in proxy solicitation expenses alone.

In July of 1955, Wolfson is once again in the spotlight and on the hot seat when Washington, D.C., bus drivers go on strike. As chairman of Capital Transit, he is called before a Senate subcommittee: Wolfson gets into a shouting match with senators who accuse him of looting the company. He replies that he believes in "being liberal" in the payment of dividends to shareholders. After the strike ends two and a half weeks later, Congress passes a bill to make Capital Transit a public entity. In contrast to the Montgomery Ward deal, Wolfson is the financial winner, selling the company for $13.5 million.

five | hero or hood?

(1956-1964)

The Junkman from Florida emerges from the Montgomery Ward and Capital Transit battles with a decidedly double-edged reputation. Large segments of the investing public see him as a Robin Hood of finance who redistributes corporate riches hoarded by entrenched management to deserving shareholders. Large segments of the general public, as well as members of the eastern establishment and their allies in Congress, see him as a hood in the criminal sense, a looter hiding behind the guise of a champion of corporate democracy. In the halcyon years from 1956 to 1964, the Junkman does plenty to feed both conflicting images.

As chairman of Merritt-Chapman & Scott, Wolfson presides over one of the nation's leading public works and defense contractors. By 1957, MCS will be ranked 9th of the Fortune 500 with an estimated value of $132 million, the equivalent of $375 million in today's dollars. On the public works side, MCS gets a $25.7 million contract to W7 build the foundations for the 5-mile span of the Mackinac Bridge connecting Michigan's Upper and Lower Peninsulas. The longest suspension bridge in the western hemisphere, the Mackinaw is hailed as direly needed. MCS also wins a $107.9 million bid to build the Glen Canyon Dam on the Colorado River in northern Arizona, an undertaking widely denounced as an environmentally invasive political boondoggle. But the company's biggest contract is a $265.2 million commission for its New York Shipbuilding subsidiary to build the USS Kitty Hawk. Designed as a state of the art aircraft carrier, the Kitty Hawk will be over a thousand feet long and almost 300 feet wide, and host 85 aircraft and a crew of 5,624 officers and men. Completion times on these projects will be three years, ten years, and five years respectively.

Meanwhile back in Jacksonville, Wolfson is becoming a Jewish liberal counterpart to the late conservative press lord William Randolph Hearst. He acquires a hometown newspaper, the Jacksonville Chronicle, and the Miami Beach Sun. Both papers editorialize in favor of civil rights, the labor movement, and efforts to aid the poor and hungry, causes that are also supported by donations from the Wolfson Family Foundation. But Wolfson's image and his future prospects take an ominous turn with yet another series of failed corporate gambits, including attempts to buy the Brooklyn Dodgers, the Washington Senators, and the Baltimore

Colts, and a bid for control of the American Motors Corporation (AMC) run by George Romney, the moderate Republican destined to become governor of Michigan.

Wolfson's bid for AMC lays the seeds for his downfall. It begins as another hostile takeover attempt rejected by shareholders. It briefly turns friendly, as Wolfson meets with Romney and pledges his support in helping to turn the company around. But as documented by St. Louis University law professor Alan M. Weinberger, Wolfson secretly sells his stake In AMC and shorts 137,000 shares of AMC stock, betting that the price will fall. As it happens, AMC rebounds under Romney's leadership, and the company's share price rises, exposing Wolfson to potentially major losses. In June 1958, his investment advisor Alexander Rittmaster plants an intentionally misleading story in the New York Times that Wolfson is selling his AMC shares. In truth, Wolfson has already sold his shares and is shorting the stock.

Thanks to the high public profile he got during the D.C. transit strike and the Montgomery Ward takeover attempt, Wolfson's dealings in AMC shares attract the attention of investigators at the Securities and Exchange Commission, who accuse him of using false information to drive down the price of the stock. Wolfson's attorneys manage to settle the case without admission of wrong doing and a pledge by Wolfson not to make any false statements about AMC or his holdings in the company. But Wolfson is now at the top of the government's watch list, a dubious distinction that will soon come back to haunt him.

Meanwhile, personal demons haunt Wolfson behind the scenes. In public, he is a mystery man, stoic and taciturn save when he was denouncing his business rivals in letters and telegrams. In private, he is a manic-depressive tyrant. He doesn't smoke or drink alcohol, but he is addicted to pills like seconal and tuinal, which he takes every night in order to go to sleep. Flo Wolfson is passive and demure, an elegantly reserved Southern belle, always faithful and supportive. Her husband's friends, however, know Lou Wolfson to be a wolf.

Wolfson and his daughter Marcia have an especially tumultuous love-hate relationship with painful incestuous undertones. When she was a little girl, her Dad called her "Shug," short for "Sugar," the term of endearment reserved for her mother, and heaps her with fatherly adoration and affection, taking her almost everywhere with him. But after she reaches the age of puberty, Lou insists that she take pills like his to go to sleep, and is very loving at times. At age 17, when she comes home from a date with a 22-year-old boyfriend, he physically beats her in front of her brothers screaming, "See what happens to you when you're bad!"

At age 18, when Marcia informs her father that she intends to marry Everett Lassman, who owns a restaurant coincidentally named "Wolfie's," Lou slaps her across the face, growling, "No one would want you! No one!" Years later, Marcia will recall, "I thought beatings like that meant love." She soon enters a sanitarium, where the doctor diagnoses her as having an "Electra complex," the father-daughter counterpart to an Oedipus complex. "Your father is sexually attracted to you, and you are in love with your father," the doctor says, adding, "But just remember, Marcia, you're not the crazy one in the family – your father is."

In 1958, ostensibly heeding his own doctor's advice to find a relaxing diversion from his financial battles, Wolfson starts taking an interest in thoroughbred horse racing. But rather than slowing down, he turns his new hobby into a business. In 1960, he buys Harbor View Farms, a 478-acre track near Ocala, a hundred miles west of Jacksonville. Over the next four years, he develops his Ocala spread into the second highest money winning stable in thoroughbred racing, making it the north Florida counterpart of horse breeding capitals like Kentucky and Maryland, and symbolically thumbing his nose once again at the WASP establishment. Then a snake in the grass rears his venomous head. In 1964, his once trusted confidante Alexander Rittmaster is convicted of bribery in connection with a bid by Rittmaster to supply marking meters to New York City. Although Wolfson reminds Rittmaster that he has "friends in high places," Rittmaster agrees to cooperate with the government in its ongoing investigations of Wolfson's financial empire in hopes of getting a reduced sentence on his bribery conviction.

six | "dear abe ..." (1965-1966)

In June of 1965, Lou Wolfson retains the services of Washington, D.C. attorney Abe Fortas, a partner in the firm of Arnold, Fortas, and Porter. It is an ostensibly routine act, an effort by a prominent businessman to obtain first rate legal counsel, but it sets the stage for a national scandal that will result in the tragic demise of both parties. Wolfson originally asks Fortas to handle two matters: (1) an outstanding $65–70 million settlement claim by MCS against the Navy in connection with building the Kitty Hawk, and (2) a recently initiated SEC investigation into irregularities in the trading of MCS stock.

In July 1965, President Lyndon Johnson offers Fortas a seat on the Supreme Court. Fortas is reluctant to accept. He is making $200,000 a year in his law practice, and he and his tax attorney wife relish the high life of

Georgetown society. Although he has known Fortas for barely two months, Wolfson offers in writing to provide Fortas with "any financial assistance he felt necessary." The politically liberal Fortas is impressed by the Wolfson Family Foundations support of civil rights; he agrees to become a paid consultant to the foundation, attend one meeting a year, and prepare promotional material for the foundation. On October 22, Wolfson attends a reception for Fortas at the Supreme Court, and joins him for dinner. The next day they meet at Fortas's home, where the future justice assures Wolfson that the SEC investigation of MCS merely involves "technical violations."

In January 1966, Wolfson sends Fortas a $20,000 check for services to the Wolfson Family Foundation in the year ahead. The following month, Fortas writes LBJ suggesting that the President see to resolving the MCS case as a "policy of non-discrimination," but LBJ does not act. On June 10, the SEC refers the MCS case to the Justice Department for criminal prosecution. Four days later, Fortas flies down to Florida, where he attends a foundation meeting, then stays overnight at Harbor View Farms. LBJ unsuccessfully tries to contact Fortas by phone from the White House. On June 21, Fortas terminates his arrangement with the foundation in a letter to Wolfson, but does not return the $20,000 payment until the end of the year.

Meanwhile, on September 19, 1966, a federal grand jury indicts Wolfson in the MCS stock trading case. The following month, the same grand jury indicts Wolfson and his close associate Elkin "Buddy" Gerber for alleged securities law violations in trading shares of Continental Enterprise, his Jacksonville-based theater management company. Assigned to soon-to-be legendary prosecutor Robert Morenthau, the Continental Enterprises case is particularly controversial because Wolfson and Gerber are charged with selling unregistered shares to the public. The ubiquitous Alexander Rittmaster, now a convicted felon, agrees to testify for the government in both cases to avoid indictment as a co-conspirator. Rittmaster also sings about Wolfson's agreement to pay Fortas a retainer through the Wolfson Family Foundation, adding still more fuel to what is already a fiery national scandal.

Insisting that he had relied on his brokers to handle details of regulatory compliance in the MCS and Continental enterprises transactions, Wolfson complains that he is being victimized for his celebrity, and being scapegoated by people threatened by his challenges to the entrenched management of large corporations. In hindsight, Henry Manne, dean of the George Mason University law school, will agree with him. "From the vantage point of a quarter of a century later, it seems clear that Wolfson had no criminal intent, that the government had come after him with guns blazing, determined to rid the business scene of a dangerous [corporate] raider," Manne declares in a 2010 law review monograph, adding, "There are no subtle shadings here; Wolfson was the victim of a zealous prosecutor." But Manne's glowing endorsement comes a quarter of a century too late for the Junkman.

seven | heartaches for the producers (1967-1968)

In early 1967, Lou Wolfson gets tragic news: his wife Flo is diagnosed with breast cancer. Despite his unfaithfulness, Wolfson is heartbroken. Several weeks later, he suffers a heart attack, as well. He requests postponements of his securities violations cases, but his pleas fall on deaf ears at the Justice Department. The Continental Enterprise case goes to trial in early September of 1967, with Rittmaster as a witness for the prosecution. Wolfson's attorney's assure him that the worst he'll receive is monetary civil penalties for minor technical offenses. But after hearing three weeks of testimony, the jury convicts Wolfson and Buddy Gerber of nineteen criminal counts of violating and conspiracy to violate securities laws by selling unregistered stock. The pair now face a possible 95 years in jail. On November 28, Judge Edmund L. Palmieri sentences Wolfson to a one-year prison term, fines him $100,000, and orders him to pay the government's prosecution costs. Wolfson vows to appeal the verdict and request a new trial.

In June of 1968, Wolfson is back in Judge Palmieri's court facing separate charges in the MCS stock trading case, with Rittmaster once again testifying for the prosecution. The charges center around an alleged sweetheart deal back in 1961 in which Wolfson allowed an associate named Joseph Koscow to purchase shares in MCS at artificially depressed prices of $8 to $12 per share and then sell them back to the company at $18.75 per share. The judge ultimately dismisses the specific securities violation charges, and instructs the jury to limit their deliberations to charges related to perjury and obstruction of justice. On August 8, the jury convicts the defendants on all remaining counts. Palmieri sets the sentencing date for December.

In the meantime, Wolfson is approached by Dr. Samuel Belkin, president of Yeshiva University in New York City. According to Wolfson's subsequent account, Belkin claims to be acting as an intermediary for Francis Cardinal Spellman, who, in turn, is a friend of Judge Palmieri. Spellman is in need of funds to finance a major lobbying effort to amend the New York State constitution to permit state aid to parochial schools. Belkin reportedly tells Wolfson that if he makes a $1 million contribution to Catholic Charities, his legal problems will be over. Wolfson is furious. "I refused to buy a political influence or any other types of influence," he will recall after the fact. "I spent $2 million fighting this injustice." By November, it is clear that the cancer in Flo Wolfson's breast is spreading to her liver, and that her condition is terminal. Wolfson requests a postponement of his sentencing, but the judges refuses him. A few days later, an even more outraged Wolfson sends Palmieri a telegram vowing "to do everything to have you removed from the bench."

Incredibly, Wolfson somehow manages to attend to his business affairs while his wife is dying of cancer and his freedom is jeopardized by criminal prosecutions. In early 1967, his son Steve brings him a script by actor Mel Brooks for a movie titled "The Producers." Brooks hopes the project will be his debut as a Hollywood director. Ironically, it is a black comedy about a sleazy theatrical producer and a sleazy accountant who want to produce a surefire Broadway flop entitled "Springtime for Hitler: A Gay Romp with Adolph and Eva at Berchtesgaden." They sell more shares in the project to investors than they can repay, planning to abscond to Brazil when the play closes. But their plans go awry when the play turns out to been improbably hit. At the 1968 Academy Awards, the film wins an Oscar for Best Writing, Story, and Screenplay.

Even as Flo is dying of cancer, the 56-year-old Wolfson's children suspect he is having an affair with Patrice Jacobs, the vivacious 31-year-old daughter of his horse trainer, while he is standing trial in New York for securities violations. His daughter, Marcia, confronts her father one evening when he returned from the courthouse to the family suite at the Pierre Hotel, where Flo was bedridden. "Dad, do you know how it makes Mother feel to know that Patrice is going to the trial with you every day?" Marcia asks, unable to resist adding, "I can read that little witch like a book." Wolfson's face clouds over and he raises his hand as if he was about to strike her, "I don't want to hear from you ever again!" he screams as she flees to an adjoining room in the hotel suite.

On December 7, 1968, Wolfson is back in federal court, where Palmieri fines him $32,000 and sentences him to serve 18 months in prison on top of his 12-month sentence in the Continental Enterprise case. The next day, Florence Monsky Wolfson dies in a hospital in Miami. "The shops on Arthur Godfrey Boulevard closed in Mother's honor, and the shopkeepers were crying," recalls her daughter Marcia Wolfson. "Daddy was inconsolable."

eight | Inmate #3302 (1969)

When Richard M. Nixon is inaugurated as the 38th President of the United States, his first priority is coping with the war in Vietnam. His second priority, according to a memoir by Nixon's top aide John Erlichman, is removing Abe Fortas, whom he regards as too liberal, from the Supreme Court. Lou Wolfson plays an indirect role in the first initiative by virtue of having constructed the aircraft carrier Kitty Hawk, which is participating in combat operations in the Gulf of Tonkin. He plays a very direct role in the second priority by virtue of his agreement to pay Fortas a retainer through his family foundation, and by continuing to seek Fortas's help even after Fortas terminated the agreement.

For Wolfson, the most pressing matter at hand concerns appeals of his conviction in the Continental Enterprises case. Claiming that a government official forged a key incriminating document on paper manufactured after the letterhead date, Wolfson gets an evidentiary hearing before Palmieri. But after eight days of testimony that includes scientific ink and paper analysis, the judge rules that Wolfson has not proven the document is forged, and denies his motions for a new trial. Wolfson's conviction is affirmed by U.S. Court of Appeals for the Second Circuit. On April 1, 1969, the US. Supreme Court denies Wolfson's petition for a writ of certiorari to reexamine the actions of the trial court and the appeals court.

On April 11, Wolfson writes a frantic letter to Fortas. "Abe, I want you to do something for me ... I cannot go to prison right now; if you could do anything to get me a Presidential pardon – have President Johnson call Mr. Nixon." Fortas does not comply with the request. Wolfson then writes to Senator Spessard Holland of Florida asking him to personally appeal to President Nixon to delay his imprisonment until he can file more appeals. On April 22, Holland asks for an appointment with Nixon, but after consulting his attorney general John N. Mitchell, Nixon turns down Holland's request.

On April 25, 1969, Wolfson enters the federal prison camp at Eglin Air Force Base in Ft. Walton Beach, Florida, where he is branded inmate #3302. On May 6, Wolfson surrenders to the Justice Department a copy of his agreement with Fortas, which shows that the $20,000 check he sent the Justice was actually just the first installment of an annual stipend for the rest of Fortas's life or to his widow for as long as she lived. Three days later, Life magazine runs a six-page story detailing Abe Fortas's connection to the Wolfson Family Foundation. That weekend, FBI agents arrive at Elgin AFB with a subpoena for Wolfson. Under questioning, Wolfson insists that Fortas never did anything to help him other than give him reassurances that his alleged securities violations were merely technical in nature.

Although Wolfson's affidavit about Fortas is exculpatory, attorney general Mitchell uses the fact that he has a statement from Wolfson to create the impression with Chief Justice Earl Warren that he is on top of a "rapidly unfolding investigation" and that "far more serious evidence" against Fortas will come out unless the embattled Justice steps down. The gambit works. On May 15, 1969, amid calls for his impeachment, Abe Fortas resigns from the Supreme Court.

Meanwhile, Wolfson adjusts to life at the minimum security prison nicknamed "Club Fed." There are tennis courts and landscaped walking trails, and most of the other 829 inmates are nonviolent white collar criminals. His daughter Marcia is staying at a nearby hotel so she can make regular visits. With time off for good behavior, Wolfson's one-year sentence is eventually reduced to nine months and one day. He also receives a rare piece of good news: in June of 1969, his former confidante turned stool pigeon Alexander Rittmaster dies of a heart attack at age 53. But Club Fed is still an enormous comedown for the formerly high flying Junkman. He will later recall the indignity of having to watch the 1969 Triple Crown races on a black-and-white prison TV set with a motley crew of "con artists, thieves, bootleggers, and draft dodgers."

nine | back on track (1970-1977)

On June 20, 1970, Lou Wolfson is released from federal prison camp, and free to resume his still unresolved legal war against the government. Although he has finished serving time for his alleged crimes in the Continental Enterprises case, the MCS case is still open. But things are looking up, at least for a few months. In the spring of 1970, the US. Court of Appeals for the Second Circuit reverses the convictions of Wolfson and his co-defendants in the MCS case on all counts, ruling that Judge Palmieri committed reversible errors including not adequately explaining to the jury that the charge of securities fraud against them had been dismissed.

Stunningly, the government proceeds to retry Wolfson two more times, ignoring the late Alexander Rittmaster for obvious reasons and the still living Buddy Gerber, Joseph Koscow, and Marshal Staub, the former president of MCS, for not so obvious reasons. Wolfson is represented by the legendary Washington, D.C. attorney and political insider Edward Bennett Williams. The second and third MCS trials end with hung juries voting in favor acquittal by 11–1 and 10–2. A fourth MCS trial is set for 1972, but Wolfson avoids it and more potential jail time by pleading no contest to one felony count of filing a false corporate statement in return for the government dropping all other charges. He is given an 18-month suspended sentence, and fined $10,000.

The final outcome of the MCS criminal cases is rumored to be the result of the unseen hands of White House officials working in Wolfson's favor for a change. By this time, attorney general John Mitchell has resigned in the wake of the Watergate scandal. But his successor Richard Kleindienst is surely aware that Wolfson cooperated with Mitchell back in 1969 when be surrendered the Wolfson Family Foundation agreement with Abe Fortas and gave a statement to FBI officials. Wolfson subsequently petitions to have MCS pay his legal expenses. In 1974, the Delaware Supreme Court issues a landmark ruling that the company must pay for expenses Wolfson incurred in defending himself against the charges that were ultimately dropped, it is small recompense. By then, Wolfson has spent $10 million on lawyers, and his financial empire is a bare shadow of what it once was.

In between the hung jury MCS trials and the no contest plea, yet another scandal involving a soon to be national celebrity erupts. The key figure in the scandal, which also relates to MCS case, is Larry King, then a Miami radio host. Wolfson and King had been close friends until King admitted that he tricked Wolfson into giving him $48,000 to pay then-incoming attorney general Mitchell in return for Mitchell reviewing Wolfson's convictions in the Continental Enterprises and MCS cases. In 1971, Wolfson files a complaint charging King with also pocketing $5,000 that was part of a 1968 payment of $25,000 intended for New Orleans district attorney Jim Garrison, who was investigating the John F. Kennedy assassination. (Wolfson's interest in the JFK investigation is unclear, but it seems he did not believe the lone-assassin conclusion made by the Warren Commission.)

King is arrested for grand-larceny, fingerprinted, and mug-shot. The criminal charges against King are eventually dropped in the wake of a court ruling that the statute of limitations has expired. Outraged by what he feels is yet another miscarriage of justice, Wolfson writes letters to King's radio station bosses declaring that King is "a menace to the public" and insisting that they pay for King's "treatment in a mental institution for six months so he can do no further harm in this community or any other." Instead, the radio station bosses simply fire King; he later resurrects himself to become a CNN personality interviewer.

Amid all this continuing drama, Wolfson becomes ever more focused on his love life and his love for thoroughbred horse racing. The two interests ultimately dovetail. In 1972, after romancing Hollywood actress Debbie Reynolds who is in a bitter divorce battle with her second husband Harry Karl, the 60-year-old Wolfson marries Patrice Jacobs. Twenty-five years younger, Patrice is the daughter of the late Hall of Fame horse trainer Hirsch Jacobs, who had won 3,596 races, more than any other trainer in the history of the sport. Wolfson's marriage to Patrice comes as something of a shock to the children of his first wife, who are not invited to the wedding and only learn about it from articles in the newspapers. That sets the stage for what will one day become a bitter estate contest.

In the meantime, Wolfson pours much of his still considerable energies into rejuvenating Harbor View Farms, identified in the racing world by its dramatic flamingo-pink and black silks. Once the second ranked money winning stable in the nation, Harbor View Farms went out of business for all intents and purposes during Wolfson's confinement in federal prison. Wolfson resumes management of his breeding and racing interests in 1971. By 1977, Harbor View Farms is the fourth ranked money winning stable in the sport, and it is poised for historic glory thanks to the birth of a colt with the legalistic sounding name Affirmed.

ten | affirmed
(1978-1979)

When the Harbor View Farms entry Affirmed steps onto the race track at Churchill Downs for the 1978 Kentucky Derby, he is as much the subject of doubts as his controversial owner Lou Wolfson. Those doubts are belied by the three-year-old's heritage. Conceived in Kentucky and born and bred in Florida, Affirmed is among over 28,000 foals born in the exceptionally strong thoroughbred class of 1975. He is the great-great-grandson of War Admiral, the 1937 Triple Crown winner whose epic rivalry with Seabiscuit will become the subject of a best-selling book and an Oscar-winning film. He is the great-great-great grandson of Man O'War, who won two of the three Triple Crown races in 1920. More to the point, he is the grandson of Raise a Native, another Wolfson-owned horse who is also the sire of his chief rival, Alydar, the bookmakers' favorite to win the Derby.

Ironically, Affirmed behaves more like Seabiscuit than mighty War Admiral or the redoubtable Raise a Native, the common ancestor he shares with Alydar. Affirmed is laid-back in demeanor, relaxed and sociable around people, and slightly undersized in physique. Alydar, by contrast, is a-hunk, large, muscular, and physically imposing. Alydar is also more popular among racing fans. The odds on Aydar are 6–5. The odds on Affirmed are only 95. But Affirmed can run with more precision, and as one expert observer notes, he has "a heart of steel and a reservoir of class" – much like his 66-year-old owner Lou Wolfson.

Why Wolfson chose to name his horse Affirmed is a question avidly speculated upon by fans and journalists alike, especially in the wake of Wolfson's legal troubles. As law professor Alan M. Weinberger points out, "As the final word of an appellate opinion which Wolfson understood would likely end his freedom, 'Affirmed' could not possibly have held a positive connotation." Wolfson himself is enigmatic on the question. When asked at press conferences, he refers to a past thoroughbred champion named Affectionately, claiming, "My wife likes 'Aff' on account of Affectionately and we've had good luck with those kinds of names so far."

Wolfson attorney Michael Goldman later claims that his client is angry at the US. Supreme Court for affirming his conviction in the Continental enterprises case, and is showing his contempt for the judicial process by metaphorically saying, "Affirmed? I'll give you Affirmed!" Wolfson's longtime personal secretary Monteen Tomberlin insists that Patrice Wolfson "gave Affirmed his name based on many important decisions, personal, business, and otherwise, that have been affirmed over the years."

None of the naming issues matter when Affirmed, with 18-year-old prodigy Stevie Cauthen in the saddle, enters the starting gates along with Alydar, and nine other thoroughbreds. Wolfson is in the stands alongside his wife and his brother, Nathan. When the starting bell sounds, Sensitive Prince, the third ranked favorite at 9–2, bolts to an early lead. Affirmed runs in third place throughout the backstretch, with Alydar staying back in the field. Entering the far turn, Affirmed moves to the lead past Wood, Memorial winner Believe It. Alydar charges for the finish line, closing fast. But Affirmed holds on, and wins by 1 1/2 lengths.

Two weeks later, Affirmed and Alydar meet again in the second leg of the Triple Crown, the Preakness Stakes at Pimlico Race Course in Baltimore, Maryland. At 1 3/16 miles, the track is slightly longer than the 1 1/4 oval at Churchill Downs, which gives an edge to Alydar. This time Affirmed sets the pace from the beginning, moving in front of Alydar and the rest of the field. Alydar makes his move on the far turn at about the same point where Affirmed took the lead in the Kentucky Derby. Affirmed has a short lead coming into the stretch, but Alydar is closing fast once again. Somehow, Affirmed holds on to win by a neck.

The final leg of the 1978 Triple Crown is held on June 10 at Belmont Park in Queens, New York. At a mile and a half, this is the longest of the three races, and once again, that gives the edge to Alydar. Coming out of the starting gate, Affirmed sets a slow pace in front of Alydar and the rest of the pack. With eight furlongs left,

Alydar's jockey Jorge Velasquez starts moving his horse alongside Affirmed. For the next six furlongs, Affirmed and Alydar run neck and neck, pulling well ahead of the rest of the field. Heading into the stretch, Alydar gets his nose in front. But just as Affirmed seems to tire, Cauthen whips him left-handed, something he had never done in eight previous rides on Affirmed - and Affirmed wins by a nose.

Affirmed's victory in the 1978 Triple Crown is historic for several reasons. He is the 11th (and as of 2013, the last) Triple Crown winner in thoroughbred racing. The 1978 Triple Crown is still the only series in which the same horses finished first and second in all three races, a testament to Alydar, as well as Affirmed. In addition to netting nearly $1 million in prize money for Harbor View Farms and making an indelible mark in the history of the sport, Affirmed's triumph provides his owner Lou Wolfson with a measure of public and personal redemption. But Wolfson himself is typically restrained in his celebration. His brother Nathan later recalls, "As Lou and I went down to the saddling ring after the race, I joked, 'That wasn't even close.' He was happy, but he wasn't emotionally overwrought. He said, 'I'm just glad nobody got hurt, the horse or the jockey.'" Affirmed is named Horse of the Year in 1978 and again in 1979.

epilogue: daddy dearest (1980-2007)

Lou Wolfson's comeback victories on the legal front and on the racetrack – as well as his previous triumphs in finance - are achieved at the expense of his family. He spends the last 29 years of his life commuting between luxury homes in Bal Harbor, Florida, Westbury, Long Island, and Saratoga Springs, New York, with his second wife Patrice. The inner demons that haunted him throughout his heyday come increasingly to the fore during his declining years. To his four children by his late wife Florence Monsky Wolfson, the period between 1979 and 2007 is both a painful flashback to times gone by, and a living nightmare dominated by the man whose daughter calls him "Daddy Dearest" because he so often behaves like a male counterpart to the infamously narcissistic Hollywood actress Joan Crawford.

Marcia Wolfson, the daughter he beat, berated, and made untoward advances upon, suffers three failed marriages, two with Everett-Lassman, whom she divorces, remarries, and then divorces again, and one with Manfred Rechtschaffen, by whom she bears a son. She later becomes a theatrical agent mostly as a ploy to meet new people, especially men, and eventually marries one of her clients, actor Daniel Drake. Wolfson's three sons, though never physically beaten like their sister, continue to reel from their father's emotional abuse.

The oldest boy, Steve, who never got credit from his father for brining in the script to an Oscar winning movie, owned horses and frequently bet in contests. Gary, the third born child, becomes an Executive in China. He moved to Santa Monica with his wife Marisa, and continues to travel China. Marty, the youngest child, is movie star handsome in his father's image. But he incurs Lou's disapproval after he poses nude in Playgirl Magazine in 1978, the year of Affirmed's victories in the Triple 5 Crown. Marty goes on to become a successful horse trainer, but he refuses to work with his father. He suffers two failed marriages, and bouts of depression that leave him vowing "never to bring a child into this awful world."

The dysfunctional Wolfson family's attempts at reconciliation are almost all for naught. At an elaborately staged family reunion in Jacksonville in 1984, Lou declines even to make a toast, and refuses to speak to daughter Marcia, who admittedly makes a fool of herself with a drunken toast in which she declares "how much I love Daddy."

The increasingly paranoid Wolfson subsequently accuses sons –"though handsome as movie stars" – Steve and Gary of being "thieves"; Dad was dead wrong. A short time later, he is diagnosed with Alzheimer's disease. In 2002, the planning for a celebration of Lou's 90th birthday in Miami threatens to turn into yet another debacle. Debbie Reynolds offers to serenade him, but Patrice warns her to not to come anywhere near her friend and suspected former paramour. Amazingly enough, when daughter Marcia arrives at the family apartment the next day to make one last attempt at reconciling with her father, the Alzheimer's afflicted Wolfson actually breaks down in tears, and tells her, "I'm sorry for what I did to you."

Ironically, the double-edged example Wolfson set as America's first corporate raider and avowed advocate of shareholder democracy inspires younger generations of swashbuckling financiers even as his health declined. In 1978, the year of Affirmed's historic triumph, a brilliant but ultimately corrupted numbers whiz named Michael Milken moves from New York to Los Angles, and opens the X-shaped trading desk in the offices of Drexel Burnham where he becomes known as the "junk bond king." In 1981, a Texas oilman T. Boone Pickens launches his first hostile tender offer for Hugoton Production, a target 30 times the size of his own Mesa Petroleum Company. In 1985, Carl Icahn announces his landmark hostile bid for air carrier TWA. In 1998, Sanford Weill successfully completes the merger between the Traveler's insurance Company and banking giant Citigroup that created a "financial supermarket," the Wall Street equivalent of the pioneering corporate conglomerate Wolfson started building at Merrill-Chapman & Scott back in 1949.

Louis Elwood Wolfson dies at home in Miami Beach, Florida, on December 30, 2007, nine days before his 96th birthday. What was once a multi-billion-dollar empire in today's monetary terms has dwindled to something on the order of $20 million. His will bequeaths the bulk of his remaining fortune to his second wife Patrice, and relative pittances to the children of his first wife Flo, sparking a bitter estate battle that will result in Marcia winning just $100,000. The New York Times, which had hailed him as one of "Today's Titans of Finance" in 1955, notes his passing with the headline, "Louis Wolfson, Central to the Fall of a Justice, is Dead at 95." That banner and the 576-word obituary beneath it do precious little justice to the bittersweet legacy of the junkman genius who revolutionized modern finance and left an indelible mark on the history of thoroughbred horse racing.

LOUIS E. WOLFSON
AGE 47

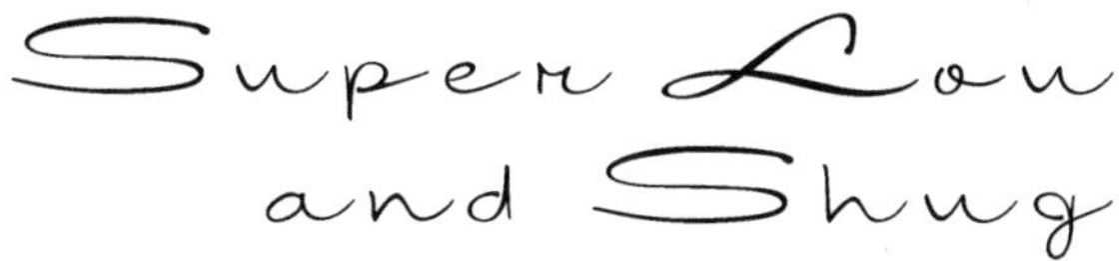

Super Lou and Shug

As a kid, I was fascinated, watching my Dad's working ways. I still find it unbelievable. My father studied financial situations. He would find a company that was losing money, investigate the problem, then invest in it. The officers that worked for him only wanted big salaries, and because of that greed expressed by his peers, he felt that stockholders should be compensated; he was also always for the underdog.

Dad was a giving, understanding, and BRILLANT businessman, operating to make sure his companies were money-making. He had an incredible mind behind his big deals. Dad was ahead of his time: A True Seer. He employed and transferred his intense feeling for others to his work, employing friends of his like Doran Weinstein -his friend, ex-football player, and my cousin. Dad sent Doran to investigate the large returns; for example, they both agreed that Washington was right for the next move. Dad spent $20 on a share for 109,000 – Capital Transit Company. Dad often found himself in uncomfortable positions from the press due to the weight of the deals he was making. Next to follow was New York Shipbuilding Company; this was a big opportunity for the company, purchased for only $2,000,000. Super Lou told the unions to up production: they did, and they ended up being worth $65,000,000. New York Ship Building bought NESCO for $35,000,000. Merit Chapman, the lead company, purchased Newport Steel for $60,000,000 which same to gross sales. Next to purchase was Devoe Reynolds for $40,000,000.

From the deals he was making, to the business he did, I still cannot believe Super Lou's Brain. In our gorgeous home on Biscayne Bay, you could find Daddy getting up at 2:00 am, calling his people talking about his deals. It is hard to believe my luck sometimes, that all of this good fortune came out of that incredible man. But as I write about Dad's business side, it makes me remember, and want to show his human side. He wasn't aloof, just very shy. He would sometimes need to hold my Mother's hand for support, and he was so generous. My Father did not smoke or drink, and no profanity was allowed. One evening, he and Mother were at a friend's home, and the host used horrible and offensive language, so he and Mother got up, and left, deciding never to speak to that friend again!

Though he was mostly unimpressed with the company he kept, as a child, I couldn't believe who he had in his life. Marilyn Monroe and Joe DiMaggio would ask him for financial advice. I was rarely allowed to see her, but Daddy said that she was very intelligent. It was odd to have the relations we did during such a difficult time, it made everything seem so much more dramatic. Joe DiMaggio was a witness at Dad's trial when he was convicted in 1968, and my mother died at same time, at only 53-years-old. I remember how Patrice Jacobs called constantly to see how Mom was, and how the kids were doing. That's when my dislike of her began, I knew she was after my Father.

How did I find out that they, Patrice Jacobs and my Dad, had wed? It was written so in Ed Sullivan's column. I was devastated, and yet not at all surprised. Her Father Hirsch Jacobs had been Dad's trainer, and Patrice, the thorn in my side, was so close to the family (and not to mention almost thirty years younger than he was). Really my Mother and I could always see right through her. It felt like an evil step-mother Cinderella story, she got everything that she wanted while his children received a pittance when he died.

Despite the rather tumultuous events, one of my fondest times in my life was when Daddy owned a movie studio. He arranged for me to spend the day with my idol, Elizabeth Taylor, and this was one of the most exciting days of my life. Elizabeth Taylor was filming the late 50's film, **The Conspirator**, and asked my Mother and I to come to the commissary. We went and ordered beautiful sweetbreads; I ate them not knowing what they were! She gave me her wedding pictures with Nicky Hilton, and I could not believe those incredible violet eyes. Daddy had so many almost unbelievable connections, he was also involved in the wildly successful **The**

Producers. Larry King was a big part of his life (trouble trouble!) We dined with John Kennedy and Jackie at the Colony. Eleanor Roosevelt had tea at our home in Miami Beach, and on and on.

I attended a wonderful party that Cobina Wright, a columnist in Beverly Hills, hosted. Dad looked sophisticated and breathtakingly handsome. He was Super Shy, so many times I saw him grimace from his shyness. He was not impressed by most of the HOLLYWOOD set, and that's probably why he was able to retain so many of their friendships. He had very sincere relationships with Joan Crawford, Debbie Reynolds, John Forsythe and Singer Dinah Shore. He enjoyed them as just normal people. We spent an afternoon with Dinah Shore and her husband George Montgomery, who showed us terrific carpentry. Debbie Reynolds and I were together at her suite in New York, where she ordered up lunch, and during our tête-a-tête, she said to me, "Patrice snatched up Louis," she took a sip of her tea, "and I thought that I could have been your Stepmother." At times, my life was so star-studded, it felt like I was looking down on my life from the sky. It was hard to grasp reality.

Dad's business side was intense and brilliant, but his human side was warm and loving, and I had a turbulent relationship with both sides. I just loved him too much! And yet, despite all that love, from age 20 to 60 I was depressed, and it felt like I lived in a Black Hole. During my time with a psychiatrist, she asked me, "Do you think that you can ever break away from this Dynasty?" adding on, "Marcia, you are not the crazy one. You're just an abnormal family caught up in a crazy World." Crazy indeed, I'm still trying to answer her question...

At Dad's funeral in 2007, I was hysterical. I said to the open coffin, which I begged the rabbi to close, questioning, exclaiming, "Daddy, why did you ruin my life?" In hindsight, it seems very dramatic, but it is how I felt.

My world has been a series of dramatic episodes. Attachments to the men that I married stemmed from my feelings for my Father, and though Mother was an absolute blessing, and my son and his children have lifted my sadness of life, I feel that writing *Super Lou* has been an eye-opening experience for me. It was an experience similar to Albert Camus' *Myth of Sysiphus*. Though writing this was a laboring experience, it's brought my some receiving some understanding, and like Sisyphus, smiling while pushing the boulder up the mountain, so I am slowly (but surely, and happily) re-finding my reasons for living.

The obituary follows these pages.

L.E.W.
Visionary
Mogul
Raider
Legend

On the theory that it's easier to make a million dollars than it is to make a thousand, Louis Wolfson parlayed A Jacksonville junkyard into a $200,000,000 industrial Empire. A Post editor reveals the inside story of

Florida's Fabulous Junkman[1]

Strange things turn men's lives in new directions and looking back on it now, Mr. Louis E. Wolfson, the Florida financier who parlayed Jacksonville junkyard into a $200,000,000 industrial empire is convinced that his fabulous career as a capitalist began one autumn afternoon in the Yale Bowl. Mr. Wolfson, a sophomore end on a University of Georgia football team that was joyously slaughtering the Elis, was playing in his first big game, an experience so heady it rendered him impetuous. On the kickoff opening the second half, he blocked a huge Yale tackle with such violence that he jarred his shoulder bones loose.

Up until that moment, Mr. Walloon, a big, quick-moving man who loved to play football more than he loved to sleep, eat or go with girls, had had one simple ambition. It was his purpose to become an All-American college end. After that he would play professional football for a decade or two. Then, when his bones grew brittle and his joints grew stiff, he would retire to some quiet coaching job where he could end his days happily amid the mall of sweat and leather, and the pleasant

1 Original Article by Harold H. Martin, "Florida's Fabulous Junk Man," *Saturday Evening Post*, July 24, 1954

sound of muscled bodies falling heavily to the turf. Unfortunately, the wounded shoulder refused to heal, and Wolfson, finally accepting the dismal fact that all college now could offer him was an education, quit school and went home to Jacksonville. There, to compensate for his blighted athletic comer, in his father's struggling scrap yard piled with rusty iron and theses-eases at junked automobiles, he set out to make vast sums of money.

The speed and ease with which he has accomplished this, not only for himself but for a happy swarm of friends and kinfolk, has dazzled Wall Street and left bewildered bankers and brokers shaking their heads groggily. It also has deeply puzzled the people who knew him in his college days. They remember him as a big, soft-spoken man, alert enough on the football field, but in the classroom the most torpid student ever to grape his way through an institution of higher learning. When he left school in his junior year he was still struggling with freshman English and history, and in economics he had never learned the basic concepts of the misses-fairs theory. In fact, his professors recall, he never even learned to spell it.

Despite his genius for making money, it is doubtful whether Mr. Wolfson, even now, at the age of forty-two, could outline lucidly the economic theories found in the textbooks. He does not need to. He has evolved a formula of his own which serves him better. The Wolfson theory is based on the simple axiom that it is easier to make a million dollars than it is to make a thousand. If you want to make 11 thousand dollars, he says, you make a little deal, and you have to be smarter than a multitude of quick-witted citizens who share the same ambition. If you want to make a million, you make a big deal, and you have to be smarter and bolder than only a handful of tycoons who can afford to play for such high stakes.

For his part Mr. Wolfson has always preferred to deal as big and boldly as possible, a policy that has paid off so prodigally for him that even in an age of murderous taxes he has become vastly rich. It has enabled him to tuck away, for himself and his children, and his brothers and their children, trust funds totaling several million dollars. It has given him oil wells, vast chunks of real estate and a chain of movie houses. It has also given him ownership of, or a controlling interest in, a half dozen multimillion dollar corporations, including huge Merritt-Chapman & Scott, a globe-girdling construction and marine salvage firm; the New York Shipbuilding Corporation, the nation's third largest shipyard; and the $23,000,000 bus-and-streetcar system which serves Washington D.C. His cash income, from salaries and dividends, runs between $500,000 and $1,000,000 a year, and for the privilege of making such money, he and his family have paid into the Federal Treasury nearly $10,000,000 in income taxes. Such success naturally has attracted considerable attention, some of it suspicious, and at one time or another Mr. Wolfson has been investigated by a Federal grand jury, a congressional committee and Senator Kefauver's crime probers. None of them have found him guilty of anything more nefarious than being smarter and more imaginative, money-wise, than most of the people he has done business with.

Sniffing Out Hidden Weaknesses

The methods by which he has accumulated for himself so large a share of the nation's wealth are, on the surface, extremely simple. The structure of the Shakespearean sonnet may have bored and battled him, but a corporation's financial report has a clear, cold beauty of form which delights him, and a depth of meaning which he is quick to comprehend. He spends hours a day, therefore, studying the financial structure of scores of companies that are listed on the big exchanges. When he finds a corporation whose stock is selling in the market at prices for below the company's true worth, he scrutinizes it closely, searching for hidden weaknesses. Most often there are sound economic reasons for the low price. Sometimes though, it turns out that a company's stock sells below par because it pays a meager dividend which does not lure investors. And this, he finds, may be due to the fact that the officers and the directors at the company themselves own little or no stock in it. They are, therefore, not interested in paying large dividends. Instead, he says, they are interested in paying themselves huge salaries and fat directors' fees, and providing for their old age with lavish pensions which may carry over to their dependents after they are dead.

When he sniffs out such a situation, which he considers shameful, he moves in swiftly. If the company fits into the pattern of the industrial empire he is building – a complex of self-supporting industries ranging from steel mills to processors of light-metals – he tucks it away as a money-maker to be kept and operated. If it is a maverick which does not conform to the pattern, he pushes its earnings as high as possible, pays out a few good dividends to enhance the value of the stock, and at the proper time sells out for a fat capital gain.

Wolfson's is the guiding brain behind each big deal, but to bring one off successfully requires a prodigious amount of detective work on the part of the associates who dig up his facts for him. Unknown in financial circles until the Wolfson star began to rise, they are a devoted retinue, made up of a onetime shoe merchant, an automobile dealer and assorted small-town lawyers, auditors and businessmen whom Wolfson has patiently trained in his methods. He chides them sharply when they err, but each of them loves him with a devotion that few capitalists receive even from their next of kin, and the strain of trying to please him has given some of them a severe case of lion to the attention of Washington's top tycoons, who yawned. Then, one evening he mentioned it, casually, to a young Atlantan, named Walter Troutman, a dinner guest in his home. Mr. Troutman, like Wolfson an ex-athlete turned financier, leaped for the telephone, calling Wolfson in Jacksonville. Wolfson sent an aide, Doran Weinstein, scurrying for a train, and the next day Weinstein phoned from Washington to say that the situation was as fraught with opportunity for rich returns as Troutman had described it. Shortly afterward, in the offices of the holding company, Wolfson paid $20 a share for 109,000 shares that were selling on the market for $18.60. So far, Wolfson and his cohorts have taken profits, in dividends or on paper, of some $6,000,000 on a $2,250,000 total investment.

Public-relations-wise, though, the deal has been a fantastic headache. The slicing of the juicy melon caused the hungry stockholders to rejoice, but it brought down upon Wolfson's head a spate of outside criticism which wounded him deeply. Newspapers denounced him, charging him with milking the company, congressional committees called him on the carpet, and the District of Columbia Public Utilities Commission, which controls his company's rate structure, chided him for asking for an increase in bus and streetcar fares in the same week he declared a large dividend from surplus funds. To which Wolfson replied patiently that the money in the surplus was earnings that should have been distributed to the shareholders long ago, and that, though it was the duty of the PUC to protect the riding public, it was his duty to protect the interests of the 2000-odd stockholders who, with him, own the company. The rate increases, he said, were for the purpose of guaranteeing them a fair return in the future. Also, he pointed out, the company's service to its riders was as good as it ever was, a statement which the commission, granting the rise in furs, did not refute.

While the storm aroused by his purchase of Capitol-Transit was still swirling around his head, Mr. Wolfson found himself in another awkward situation. He was called to explain to the Kefauver Committee why he had contributed $160,000 to the campaign of the Hon. Fuller Warren, who was elected governor of Florida in 1948. The amount, said Mr. Wolfson in reply was actually somewhat in excess of $150,000-and the reason he made such a heavy contribution was simple. He had been Warren's friend for years. He considered him the world's greatest salesman. As governor, he could clean up the gambling and other activities which gave Florida a bad name, and so publicize the state that it would enter a period of prosperity hitherto unknown. Since he and his brothers had about $7,000,000 worth of real estate and other holdings in Florida, he stood to profit, indirectly, by any actions of Mr. Warren's that would help the state as a whole. All he wanted of Warren was that he should be a good governor.

Cynical men may look askance at this statement, but those who know the warm affection in which Wolfson holds his friends, and his willingness to back them in their enterprises with great sums of money, accept it as truth. So, evidently, did Senator Kefauver.

Later, when he was campaigning for the presidential nomination, he asked Wolfson to serve on his national advisory committee. Wolfson declined. After the tempest over the Warren gift, he had resolved never again to support a political figure with anything more tangible than his vote.

Wolfson's anguish over the bad press he was receiving was soon assuaged by his discovery of another fantastic business opportunity. The New York Shipbuilding Corporation, another Victor Emmanuel outfit, had been losing money for several years, and its stock was selling at far below its book value.

Scenting another rich opportunity, Wolfson moved feet. He acquired working control of the enterprise which does about $65,000,000, gross sales, a year, for $2,000,000, and placed two of his aides in top management. To Wolfson, New York Ship's weakness lay in the simple fact that too many people were doing too little work, and he bluntly told the unions they'd have to up production or he'd liquidate the yard. They did, and

New York Ship, which had lost $194,000 in 1962, earned $3,200,000 in 1963 and a 50 per cent stock dividend was declared. Since then, Wolfson, has expanded rapidly. Through New York Ship he has bought Nesco, a $35,000,000 Milwaukee firm manufacturing a number of light-metal products, and the Somerville Iron Works at Chattanooga. Merritt-Chapman & Scott has bought NewPort Steel, a $60,000,008 (gross sales) Indiana corporation, one stock-trading deal, and Fitz Simons & Connell, a Midwestern dredge-and-dock company. Nesco has also bought out an $8,000,000 rival, and in a series of small deals Wolfson hue picked up a trio of email steel producers. Wolfson's latest acquisition is Devoe & Reynolds, a 200-year-old paint manufacturing firm doing a net business of some $49,000,000 a year.

He is at the moment busy fitting these new acquisitions into a network of diversified industries which can mutually support one another. Huge M.-C. & S. is the core of the group, and the idea is for NewPort to produce heavy steel which New York Ship can fabricate for the big construction company, while the smaller steel producers turn out light metals for Nesco. Once he gets his organization integrated, Wolfson believes that it can survive a depression with ease. In the event of a crash, he feels, it will benefit from most of the pump-priming measures the Government will try – such as the construction of hogs public works and housing projects.

Wolfson, who stays as far away from Wall Street as possible, guides his enterprises and dreams up new deals from a pleasant, sunny room in one wing of his $600,000 home on Biscayne Bay at Miami Beach. On a normal day he is at his desk from seven A.M. to midnight, filling long yellow pads with columns of figures, and he interrupts his work only to play catch with his kids when they come home from school or to roll on the floor with the youngest ones in a brief rough-house at night.

When a deal is about to hatch, he finds it difficult to sleep, and he gets up at two A.M. and goes downstairs to pore over sheets of figures. During these predawn sessions he frequently phones his associates, rousing them from their beds, and he is always puzzled when they respond foggily to his questions.

The normal relaxations which most men seek in Florida, such as golf, fishing and basking on the sand, don't interest Wolfson. He hates the taste of alcohol, and when, on doctor's orders, he takes a drink before dinner to whet his appetite, he gulps it down neat, making a face as if he were drinking castor oil.

He also dislikes the swirling social life of Miami Beach, and when, on rare occasions, he does go to a party, he stands around morosely, glancing furtively at his watch and taking little part in the chatter. He spends all his time with his wife, a Montgomery, Alabama, merchant's daughter, and his three youngsters, except for the ten-day trip he makes each month to Washington and New York to preside at directors' meetings.

Those outside the inner circle considers him aloof and cold, but he is, his friends say, merely shy. To anyone with whom he can establish any common ground or interest, such as old football players or distant kinsmen, he is extremely cordial. He has a peculiar faith in the probity and business judgment of ex-athletes, and likes to go into ventures with them. He is a partner with Allie Reynolds, the Yankee pitcher, in a chain of oil wells, and was once associated with Frank Leahy, the former Notre Dame coach, in an insurance business. He attempted to buy the Baltimore Colts, a professional football team, for Wally Butts, the Georgia coach, but the deal fell through when Butts refused to leave his college job. He also sought, without success, to buy the Washington Senators.

Wolfson is easily touched for a loan and has been known to pull $1000 out of his pocket to stake a waiter who wanted to open a small restaurant of his own. Once, after reading in a Miami paper the story of an old lady who was trying, with her own hands, to build a small church in South Miami, he gave his chauffeur, Philip Puglisi, $5000 and told him to see that the job was finished. These small gifts are personal and have nothing to do with the greater largess distributed by the Wolfson Foundation, setup as a memorial to his father, which is now building a $300,000 children's clinic for the Baptist hospital at Jacksonville.

"If I can afford to lose five thousand shooting dice, which I sometimes do," Wolfson says, "surely I can soothe my conscience by passing out a thousand or so to somebody who needs help." He also insists that his partners soothe their consciences by contributing at least 15 per cent of their income to charity.

Figures soothe and relax him, and he is happiest and most content when he is working out a complicated deal. He has long since made all the money he and his family will ever need, he says, and he now works only for the excitement of matching wife with the best brains in the country.

"I've always wanted to be a champion in everything I did," he says, "and to be a champion in business takes more brains and guts and hard work than any other job. If a man is a champion in business, and if at the same time he is honest and humble, and has a feeling of compassion for his fellow man, he can do a lot of good in the world."

Wolfson at the moment has a strong compulsion to do the world good by pointing out what he considers some fatal errors in the American business scene. The very weaknesses which have enabled him to build up his huge fortune, he believes, are destroying public confidence in business management. Venture capital that should be at work creating new jobs for people is lying dormant, he says, because the man with a little money to invest is convinced that management does not have his interests at heart. He sees labor fighting for its goals, and management fighting to protect its perquisites – its big salaries and stock options and its pension piano-but there is nobody, he insists, fighting to assure the stockholder a fair return on his money.

In a speech before the New York financial writers last March, Wolfson spelled out these views and suggested some drastic cures. (A good many sound and successful businessmen do not approve the measures be advocated.) Every officer of a company, Wolfson declared, should be required to invest at least a year's salary in the company's stock, and he should not have the privilege of buying this stock below the market price. Officers' salaries should be set low, and their main stipend should come as a reward for exceptionally good management, in the form of bonuses paid from extra profits. Pension plans should be limited, and no pension plan at all should go into effect unless it is approved by 75 percent of the stock-holders. And, he added, the stock ex-changes should have the power to de-list any company which failed to pay a dividend for two years if during those years its top officers received salaries of more than $50,000 a year.

Wolfson's strong defense of the rights of the investor might indicate that he has little sympathy with the aims of labor. This, however, does not seem to be the case. His goal, he says, is to pay the highest wages, and provide the best working conditions in industry, to men who will give him an honest day's work. One of his warm friends, strangely, is labor's stern champion John L. Lewis.

Much of Wolfson's thought of late has been devoted to working out some sort of formula which would give to labor, management and stockholders alike a share in industry's profits which would be fair to all. Already, in his own companies, he has instituted the reforms he suggested above – the first step, he believes, toward creating the kind of labor-management-capital team he has in mind.

Meanwhile, though, he is happily going ahead with plans to add to his empire any corporate weak sister which, by following other practices, has left itself vulnerable. On the desk in his office is a big black book which no outsider has ever been allowed to examine. In it are detailed records on the operations and the policies of half a dozen corporations, large and small, which he intends to add to his own holdings in the next few years. If he gets his hands on them, and he is determined that he shall, he will then be the boss of a $500,000,000 chain of industries that stretch from coast to coast.

Few who know him well would bet that he will fail in this ambition.

"The way I see it," said one Wall Streeter who has studied his methods closely, "he'll either work himself to death in the next five years, or in the next ten he'll be the biggest financial figure we've seen in a generation."

THE END

louis
e. wolfson

Obituary

WOLFSON Financier, philanthropist, and sportsman, Louis E. Wolfson, passed away December 30, 2007, at home one month before his 96th birthday. Wolfson was the son of Eastern European Immigrants, Morris D. and Sarah Goldberg Wolfson who, after living a for brief periods in Baltimore, MD and St. Louis, MO, settled in Jacksonville, FL. It was there that the 'Wolfson' name would become synonymous with humanitarianism and major philanthropies in areas as diverse as health-care, poverty, civil rights, education, and athletics. Numerous structures in Jacksonville today are living testaments to the charitable work of Lou Wolfson and his family.

Wolfson attended the University of Georgia on a football scholarship but his promising athletic career and desire to play football were cut short by a shoulder injury. He went to work at his father's scrap metal yard in Jacksonville and helped build a successful family business that carved a niche for himself as a true visionary in the history of American business. From the modest Florida Pipe and Supply, Wolfson acquired shipyards in Jacksonville and Tampa, successfully took over the D.C. Transit System in the Nation's capital, battles for control of mail order giant, Montgomery Ward, and eventually became the head of the country's first corporate conglomerate, Merritt Chapman and Scott, the construction giant responsible for building bridges, tunnels, ships, and dams throughout the world. In a 1955 New York Times article, entitled "Today's Giants in Finance," Wolfson was listed along with such legendary business figures as H.L. Hunt and Howard Hughes.

In addition to being the family patriarch, Wolfson's counsel was sought by corporate leaders, political figures and famous celebrities. He was very supportive of George Romney's entry into the compact car production vis a vis American Motors manufacture of the first compact car in the U.S. He was a consultant to the Universal Marion Corporation, which through its subsidiary, Marion Power Shovel, manufactured the still-utilized NASA crawler shuttle transporter. And, in 1968 Universal Marion Corporation co-financed the production of Mel Brooks' Oscar-winning first motion picture, "The Producers," later to become the most successful play in Broadway history.

During the late 1960's, Wolfson fought constant battles with the federal government when he was convicted of selling unregisterd securities in what was the first criminal prosecution of its kind at that time. Wolfson maintained his innocence over the years; claimed to be the victim of selective prosecution; and tried unsuccessfully through the courts to overturn his conviction. After serving 10 months in minimum security facility, Wolfson became an outspoken critic of the American penal system and an ardent proponent of meaningful reforms. During this period, Wolfson also returned to a lifelong passion, thoroughbred racing and breeding. Wolfson's Harbor View Farm, established in 1959, was among the country's leading racing and breeding operations throughout the 1960's. But it was during the 1970's that Wolfson and his homebred champion, AFFIRMED, reached the pinnacle of the sport by capturing the coveted Triple Crown in 1978. Affirmed was twice voted Horse of the Year (1978, '79) and went on to become a successful sire of mare, Flawlessly. Affirmed's Triple Crown feat has not been replicated for the past 29 years.

Wolfson is predeceased by his wife of 32 years, Florence Monsky Wolfson. He is survived by his wife of 35 years, Patrice Jacobs Wolfson, the daughter of the legendary horseman, Hirsch Jacobs; daughter, Marcia; sons Steve, Gary, and Marty; grandchildren Risa, Stephen, Fara, Jill, Alan, Caeli, Gregory, Jonathan and Justin; great-grandchildren Alexa, Libi, Pablo, Silvio and Ronit; and brothers, Cecil, Saul and Nathan. Family members and close friends say that Louis E. Wolfson never lost sight of his modest roots and was motivated by a desire to give back something meaningful to the country that provided opportunity for him and his parents.

He will best be remembered by those who knew him for his brilliant mind, business acumen, extraordinary work ethic, great commission, major philanthropies, and unparalleled humanitarianism. Funeral services will be held at 2 P.M. January 3, 2008 at Congregation Ahaveth Chesed (The Temple), 8727 San Jose Boulevard, with Rabbi Michael Matuson officiating and internment following in Temple Cemetery (in Evergreen Cemetery). In lieu of flowers, donations can be made to the Baptist Wolfson's Children's Hospital, 800 Prudential Drive, Jacksonville, Florida 32297; or the Louis E. and Patricia J. Wolfson Foundation, P.O. Box 4, Jacksonville, FL 32201. Arrangments are by Hardage-Giddens Funeral Home, 4115 Hendricks Avenue. Please sign the guestbook @ Jacksonville.com

Published in the Florida Times-Union from Jan. 2 to Jan 3, 2008

REMEMBER

Steve
Marcia
Jan. 19
Gary
WOLFSON FAMILY
Jan. 1953

how to get your man cook book

By
Marcia Wolfson

A THE HOW-TO-GET-YOUR-MAN COOKBOOK is a fascinating and practical book designed to help the "modern girl' do just that-through the medium of its Easy Recipes for Bachelorettes.

In an engaging and witty style, Marcia Wolfson shows the single girl how she, too, with just a little effort, and this book, can get her man. Moment with her culinary expertise, Marcia Wolfson demonstrates the easy way to make simple meals look complicated–and ravishingly edible.

Are you the type who can't even boil water without setting off another Johnstown Flood? Do you have rubber fingers or five thumbs? Never fear! This book stresses the easy way to prepare impressive, good-tasting meals from ordinary ingredients readily available in your neighborhood supermarket or corner grocery store.

Are you a slowpoke? Take courage – the author shows you just how quick and easy it is to whip up a delicious meal according to her tried-and-true methods.

Yes, with THE HOW-TO-GET-YOUR-MAN COOKBOOK, you too can win the final battle of your personal sexual revolution. What are you waiting for? Devour a copy of this revolutionary handbook now before it is outlawed by the dominant power group whose members are its natural victims.